It Takes two

KAREN WALLACE and ROSS COLLINS

W

This is a book about twos. It's about hes and shes.

2

Because that's how life begins. It Takes Two!

4

Sometimes he is much bigger than she is.

A bull elephant seal is as long as
a big car and weighs more than
a small tractor.
He's famous for his bad temper.

A cow elephant seal is smaller
and much gentler, too!

Sometimes **she** is much bigger than **he** is.

An angler fish lives deep down in the sea. Her mate is only a bit bigger than a tadpole.

6

A pink crab spider hardly notices her tiny partner. Would you if you were her?

A queen termite lays 30,000 eggs a day. She is as long as your hand and so **FAT** she cannot move.

A king termite is as tiny as a wasp.

Some animal pairs
look completely different
which is how **she** notices
him in the first place.

How could she ignore him? This mandrill's face almost glows in the dark!

Sometimes **he** makes sounds
to send messages to her.
He hopes that **she**
is listening.

A howler monkey

HOWLS

Phoo

A kakapo stands in the middle of the forest and makes a sound like blowing over the top of an empty bottle.

A grasshopper rubs his legs together.

Sometimes he leaves smells to send messages and mark his territory. He hopes that she will notice.

A skunk's scent is sooooooo smelly he uses it to send messages and also to protect himself from danger.

DOGS OFTEN CHOOSE LAMP POSTS TO LEAVE THEIR MESSAGE.

A ring-tailed lemur does a handstand and sprays a tree with his scent.

He and she fireflies send their messages at night.

They
FLASH
to find
a mate.

Sometimes **he** makes the nest. When it's ready **she** lays her eggs and looks after them.

A weaverbird is an amazing nest builder. He knots pieces of grass and weaves them into different shapes. Some nests are round with a hole on one side. Some nests even have tunnels.

A wren builds several nests.
He picks the strangest places.
She chooses her favourite
and pads it
with feathers.

A little ringed plover
scrapes a hollow in
bare ground.
She then lines it
with pebbles
and stalks.

17

Sometimes when **she** lays the eggs, **he** keeps them in a special place and looks after them.

Baby seahorses grow inside a pouch in their father's body. The pouch bursts open when they are ready to swim away.

18

A glass frog hides with his eggs in the leaves above jungle streams. When the eggs hatch, the tadpoles drop into the water

SPloosh.

An emperor penguin holds the egg on his feet and keeps it warm against his body. For two months he stands in the

FReeZiNg cold.

19

Sometimes **he** builds the nest and **he** looks after the eggs. **She** only lays them!

A Japanese fighting fish builds a nest of bubbles. He carries each egg up to the nest before she has a chance to eat them!

20

An Australian brush turkey buries the eggs in a nest that looks like a compost heap. If they get too hot, he uncovers them. If they get too cold, he covers them up.

A lily-trotter bird makes a floating nest on a swamp. He hatches the eggs and looks after the chicks.

Many birds share the work and stay together for life. **He** and **she** even look the same!

Albatrosses take turns to fly thousands of kilometres to find food for their chick.

Blue-footed boobies share the job of keeping their egg warm.

22

A father hornbill seals his mate into a hollow tree with mud while she sits on the eggs.

He brings her food and pushes it through a tiny hole.

23

Mammal babies suck their mothers' milk so it is not surprising that **she** does most of the work as they grow.

A mother raccoon teaches her babies to wash the river clams they like to eat.

A mother chimpanzee picks fleas from her daughters fur to keep her healthy.

Cheetah kittens are born blind and helpless. Their mother feeds them and later teaches them to hunt for themselves.

Not all mammals leave the job of looking after the young to the mother. Sometimes he helps out a little.

A father fox brings food to the cubs when they are too young to catch it themselves.

Marmosets and tamarinds almost always have twins so the father helps carry the babies.

A father hyena looks after his young when their mother is hunting.

27

If you think this book is just about animals, YOU ARE WRONG!

Helpful information

Angler fish (page 6) the tiny male is like a worm. When he finds his mate, he attaches himself and stays there.

Cheetah (page 25) a mother cheetah must protect her cubs from male cheetahs.

Chimpanzee (page 24) a mother also grooms her daughter to help form a special friendship between them.

Emperor penguin (page 19) while the male keeps the egg warm, the baby is growing inside.

Fireflies (pages 14-15) can flash because of a glowing chemical in their bodies.

Hatching (pages 18-19, 21, 22-23) a bird sits on its eggs to keep them warm, so the babies inside can grow and hatch from their shells.

Howler monkey (page 10) a howler monkey also howls to warn others of danger.

Kakapo (page 11) this rare New Zealand parrot is awake only at night.

Pink spider crab (page 7) the tiny male crab has to be very careful because his mate would eat him if she gets the chance.

Sea Horse (page 18) the female gives all her eggs to the male who keeps them inside his body until they are ready to be born.

To Willy Bullough with thanks – KW
For Charlie – RC

This edition 2014

First published by Franklin Watts,
338 Euston Road, London NW1 3BH

Franklin Watts Australia,
Level 17 / 207 Kent Street, Sydney NSW 2000

Text © 1997 Karen Wallace
Illustrations © 1997 Ross Collins
Notes and activities © 2004, 2014 Franklin Watts

Series editor: Paula Borton
Art director: Robert Walster
Consultant: Dr Jim Flegg

A CIP catalogue record is available from the British Library.
Dewey Classification 591.56
Printed in China

ISBN 978 1 4451 2891 7

Franklin Watts is a division of Hachette Children's Books,
an Hachette UK company. www.hachette.co.uk